INTRODUCTION
BUSINESS

Janet Cook

Consultant editor: Geoff Wood
Designed by Sue Mims

Edited by Judy Tatchell

Computer programs by Chris Oxlade and Bill Rivers

Illustrated by Adam Willis, Guy Smith, Sue Stitt, Roger Stewart, Martin Newton, Brenda Haw, Chris Lyon and Kuo Kang Chen

WITH COMPUTER PROGRAM LISTINGS

Contents

First published in 1985 by
Usborne Publishing Ltd, 20 Garrick Street,
London WC2E 9BJ, England.
Copyright © 1985 Usborne Publishing.
The name Usborne and the device ☙ are
Trade Marks of Usborne Publishing Ltd. All
rights reserved. No part of this publication
may be reproduced, stored in a retrieval
system or transmitted in any form or by any
means, electronic, mechanical,
photocopying, recording or otherwise,
without the prior permission of the
publisher.

Printed in Spain D.L.B. 27517-1985

About this book

You may know very little about business apart from everyday events like buying from a shop, seeing lorries carrying goods, eating at a restaurant, and so on. In fact, you cannot live in a modern society without coming into contact with many different sorts of business. This book provides an inside view of the business world.

The book shows how a business can grow from a market stall. It describes all the processes involved in running a successful business, for example researching whether it will work, financing it, selling your product or service, doing accounts, and so on.

Towards the end of the book, you enter the world of big business. There is a look at the Stock Exchange, explaining what it means when a company goes public. You can also find out about business empires and how they are built, and there are some success stories of well known businesses.

Many people who are thinking about setting up businesses are put off by terms such as profit and loss, cash flow, balance sheets, assets and liabilities. On pages 46-47 there is a glossary which gives explanations of these and many other business terms in a clear, straightforward manner.

Throughout the book you will find a number of puzzles to do with setting up and running a business. The answers to them are on page 47. Also at the end of the book there are some simple computer programs. They will enable you to test your skills at buying and selling stocks and shares, running a coffee stall, and making policy decisions in the running of a clothing business.

If you have access to a computer, type the programs in and try them. They will work on the Commodore 64, VIC 20, Apple, TRS-80 Colour Computer*, BBC, Electron, MSX and Spectrum.

3

*Extended BASIC version

What is business?

Business is based on common sense. People concentrate on doing certain things that they are good at. They then exchange their work for money, which can in turn be exchanged for the goods or services which they require. This is much more efficient than if each person worked purely to satisfy his or her own needs. There are many different types of business in the modern world. They range from very small ones to enormous multinational companies.

Coal mining and oil extraction.

Trade, service or production?

Every business either provides a service, produces goods, or buys and sells goods and services for a profit (this is called trading). Many are involved in all three activities.

The picture below shows the main areas of business going on around you every day. See if you can work out which of the three activities each business entails.

The hotel and catering business.

Financial services such as banking and insurance.*

Retail businesses (shops) which sell goods. The word retail comes from the French word *retailler* meaning to cut again. Can you think why? (Answer on page 47.)

Communications businesses such as telephone, mail and courier services.

Transportation businesses which move materials, products and people from place to place by road, rail, sea and air.

"Small" businesses

About 90 per cent of all businesses are "small"; that is, they employ less than 200 people if they are in manufacturing, or less than ten people for any other business (e.g. retail). About 3,000 small businesses are set up every week in the United Kingdom alone. The next few pages will show you the steps involved in setting up a business of your own.

Public services such as police, fire brigade, armed forces, and local and central governments. These are different from other business activities because in most countries people buy them indirectly by paying taxes.**

4

*See pages 10-11 and 23.
**See pages 24-25 for more about tax.

Electricity generation and water supply.

Construction businesses which build houses and roads, for example.

Manufacturing businesses which produce and sell goods, e.g. clothes, cars and food. The word manufacture comes from the Latin *manu factum* meaning made by hand.

Food producing activities such as farming and fishing.

Miscellaneous services including those provided by lawyers, accountants, architects, estate agents, hairdressers and entertainers.

The story of business

In ancient times, business was done by exchanging. A farmer might exchange corn for goats, or sheep for cattle. This is called bartering. But this caused problems when, say, someone had a surplus of goods that no-one needed at that time.

People started to exchange goods and services for tokens that could be stored and exchanged later. The first tokens were shells, sharks' teeth and large stones.

At one time the Romans used cattle as money, hence the word pecuniary which comes from the Latin word *pecus* meaning cattle. See if you can find out the modern meaning of pecuniary.

Later still, gold, silver and copper coins were used. To make them widely accepted, Ancient Greeks put the heads of their gods on the coins and Romans used likenesses of their emperors.

Paper money was first issued in China in about AD650 but was not introduced in Europe until the seventeenth century. It was popular because it was easier to carry than large amounts of heavy coins.

Nowadays, many commercial transactions are done through the banking system without money ever actually changing hands. Financial information is beamed across the world via satellites.

Researching a business

The most important first step for any person thinking about setting up a business is to make sure that they are choosing one which will work. This involves a thorough investigation into the customers' needs. For example, however good you are at car mechanics, your car service will not succeed if very few people in your area actually own cars, or if there is a good local garage which people already use.

On these two pages you can find out the sort of questions you should ask yourself and others in your research.

Choosing a business

It is useful to look at a range of different businesses, rather than picking the first idea that comes into your head. Study existing products and services and see whether you could do better. Then make a list of possible business ventures.

Now investigate each idea more thoroughly. Philip, for example, is thinking about setting up a window cleaning business. Before going out to buy ladders and cloths, he walks around his neighbourhood knocking on doors and asking questions.

Being tactful

It is important to ask your questions in the right way, otherwise you may not get truthful answers. For example, people may not want to admit that they cannot afford to have their windows cleaned, so Philip could ask, "How much would you pay to have your windows cleaned?"

Gaining experience

It is a good idea to gain experience before setting up on your own. Offer to provide your service free for family and friends and ask for suggestions on how you could improve. If you are going to supply a product, make things as presents or sell them cheaply to friends. See which are the most popular and offer to make things to order.

Philip is able to get a part-time job with a window cleaner. After a few months he writes a list of the pros and cons of a window cleaning business.

PROS

Not much competition in my area.
Doesn't need much money to start up.
Could also clean people's cars, or do other odd jobs for them once I get to know them. Also, a possibility of diversifying into cleaning factory and shop windows, or office cleaning and other services.

CONS

Physical risks. What would happen if I fell off a ladder and broke a leg? I could be out of action for weeks.
Not much profit in cleaning house windows.
Seasonal fluctuation – fewer people want their windows cleaned in the winter.
Not an essential service, so if incomes drop people could do without.
People are often out when I call, or have no money in the house, so I have to call again for payment.

Weighing it up

After you have studied a few business ideas carefully you will be in a position to decide which is the best proposition. Some need lots of money to start; some need special expertise; with some, location is crucial (retailing, for example). Remember to take all these factors into account in making your choice.

Planning the business

You can now make a detailed plan of your most promising business idea. Ask yourself questions like those on the list below. It does not matter if you are not actually going to set up the business at the moment – it is still fun to plan. Good business people are always assessing their businesses in this way, and adapting them as the market changes.

★ What kinds of customers am I aiming to serve – householders or business people, young or old, rich or not-so-rich?
★ How many potential customers are there in the area I aim to cover?
★ How will I attract customers?
★ What products or services will I offer?

Will you make a profit?

Once you have decided on a business scheme which your market research suggests will be successful, you can find out whether you will make a profit. To do this, you need to estimate your costs (how much it will cost you to run the business) and your pricing (how much you can sell your goods or services for).

What are your costs?

Your business costs can be broken down into four different areas: material costs, labour costs, overheads and your own wages. Decide on a time period (say, three months) and work out each of your costs for that period as shown in this picture.

Own wages

This is the minimum amount of money you feel you can live on – remember, unless you have another job you will probably not have any other income coming in.

Material costs

If you are making a product, you will need to buy the materials. Suppose you were thinking of making clothes to sell. First estimate the number of garments you will sell in three months, then work out how much cloth, thread and so on you will need. Remember to include all the tiny items like buttons, as they add up when you make a lot of garments.

Don't forget to allow for waste; mistakes can easily be made in the cutting or sewing.

Calculating the total cost

You can now work out the average cost of each item or, if you are offering a service, the cost of each hour of your work.

1. Add together the costs of your own wages, extra labour and overheads.

2. Divide this total by the number of items you expect to sell, or, if you are supplying a service, the number of hours you expect to be able to charge for.

3. If you are making a product, add this to the estimated costs of material for each item.

What price?

Base your prices on what people have said they would pay for your service, or the price of comparable goods in the shops. Remember if you sell to shops that they will probably add at least 30 per cent for their profit.

If your cost figure is higher than the price you feel you can charge, then you should rethink your business plan. Aim to make at least 10 per cent profit.

*You can find out about some of the responsibilities you have towards employees on page 23.
**See pages 10-11.

Labour costs

If you think there will be more demand for your work than you can do yourself, you will need to take on an assistant.* There are many things to take into consideration when estimating how long a job will take such as coffee breaks, giving or receiving instructions, travelling time and dealing with customers. All this can work out at about 15 to 25 per cent on top of the time it takes to perform the task itself.

Estimate how many hours you will need an assistant to put in. You can find out the hourly rate you should be paying from advertisements for similar jobs in newspapers.

Overheads

Overheads are charges incurred in the general running of the business. They include rent, rates, telephone bills, postage, fuel, advertising, insurance, travel, interest on borrowed money** and money spent on the upkeep of equipment. They do not have a direct connection with the actual product which is being made or service being provided. Estimate each bill, and any others you can think of, by talking to other people who have already set up in business.

Sasha's dressmaking

Here is a puzzle to help you see how to cost a business idea.

Sasha estimates that in three months she could sell 150 dresses at 25 tokens each. Using the information on the right, can you work out whether she would make a profit?

Material for one dress—10 tokens
Thread, buttons and zip—1 token
Own wages for three months—900 tokens
Wages for assistant—100 hours at 8 tokens an hour
Telephone bill for three months—60 tokens
Postage—10 tokens
Electricity bill for three months—50 tokens
Advertising—10 tokens
Insurance for three months—5 tokens
Bank charges for one month—20 tokens
Repairs to and upkeep of equipment—5 tokens

Borrowing money

You will probably be short of money when you set up your business and will need some help in financing it. Below, you can find out how to calculate the amount of money you need to borrow by drawing up a plan called a cash flow chart. There are also suggestions on where you might find a willing lender.

What is cash flow?

Money does two things in a business – it comes in and it goes out, rather like water in a bath. This is called cash flow. If money comes in faster than it goes out, the business is said to be more "liquid", and money is available for expansion or investment. But if money goes out faster than it comes in, the business can dry up.

	JAN	FEB
MONEY IN FROM SALES	50	75
MONEY OUT, INCLUDING YOUR TOTAL DAY-TO-DAY COSTS, AND THE COST OF EQUIPMENT	1050	250
MONEY IN MINUS MONEY OUT	⁻1000	⁻175
DIFFERENCE BETWEEN MONEY IN AND MONEY OUT SO FAR IN THE PERIOD	⁻1000	⁻1175

Borrowing from a bank

This involves preparing a campaign to convince the bank manager that your business is a good investment. This is especially important if you are under 18 because legally the bank cannot force you to pay your debts if your business goes bust. Some banks, however, are keen to encourage young people to set up businesses. Below are the sorts of things which will help you.

Cash flow chart. **Samples of your work.** **Expected sales figures.**

The bank manager may also ask you to provide him with security (a promise that you will sell a valuable possession to pay off your debts if things go wrong), or a guarantor (a friend or relative who agrees to repay the loan if you cannot).

There are two different ways in which you may be able to borrow money from a bank.

1. Overdraft*

This enables you to take out more money than you have in your account. The bank manager will give you a limit up to which you can borrow. You pay interest** on the amount you borrow on a daily basis, so you can pay back some of the money when your cash flow improves and stop paying interest on it. However, the bank manager can ask you to repay your overdraft at any moment.

2. Loan

This is safer than an overdraft because you and the manager agree the period over which you will repay the loan at the outset. However, you pay interest on the whole loan even if you do not need all of it.

10

*Overdrafts are only available in certain countries.
**Interest is a percentage of the loan which you are charged on top of the money you pay back.

Cash flow charts

You can predict how much money will be flowing in and out of the business at any given time by drawing up a cash flow chart like the one below. This will show you how much money you will need to borrow, and for how long.

In May, the chart shows that there is the same amount of money coming in as there is going out. After this, there is gradually more money coming in. As the business takes off, it should be possible to pay back the money you have borrowed

Why is there so much money going out in the first month?

Try drawing up a cash flow chart for a business idea of your own.

MAR	APR	MAY	JUNE
125	200	250	280
250	250	250	250
⁻125	⁻50	0	30
⁻1300	⁻1350	⁻1350	⁻1320

Borrowing from friends

You may have relatives or friends who can lend you money. Keep the arrangement businesslike by drawing up a written agreement showing the amount you have borrowed, what interest you will pay, and when you expect to repay the money.

Grants

Many grants are available to encourage and help small businesses. Check to see whether you qualify for one at your local government offices. Grants are a free gift of money which you do not have to pay back.

Wot, no money?

Even if you find that no-one will lend you money, there are many businesses which need very little cash at all. For example, if you sell by mail order,* you get cash with the order, so the cash flow situation is better. Also, service businesses can cost you little more than your time.

Credit is when you buy the goods with an IOU slip, promising to pay for them at an agreed time.

Some suppliers may be prepared to give you credit for bulk orders of ready-made goods. You can sell them for cash at a higher price; people are often prepared to pay for convenience. This will give you the funds to pay the supplier.

*See page 14 for more about mail order.

Establishing your business

Before you can start your new business, there are a number of decisions you still have to make. For example, who should you buy your supplies from? What premises will you work from? How much control do you want to keep in the business? This last question depends upon whether you decide to work as a sole trader, a partnership or a limited company.

The information on these two pages will help you make the right decisions for your particular business idea.

Choosing suppliers

All businesses need supplies of some sort; even services need stationery. Go to several suppliers and then compare their terms and the quality of their service before you place an order.

Suppliers may be hesitant about giving credit to a new business, so you must expect to pay cash at first. If you have your own transport, you may find it cheaper to buy from a cash and carry store as you will not have to pay for delivery.

Remember to check deliveries against your orders and invoices.*

Sole trader

EXPLANATION

You alone have responsibility for the business. You also take all the profits, after paying income tax on them.**

ADVANTAGES

1. You do not have to disclose details of your financial affairs except to the tax authorities (and the Customs and Excise if you are registered for Value Added Tax).**
2. You have the final say in any decisions that affect the company.

DISADVANTAGES

You alone are personally responsible for any business debts; if necessary, your personal possessions could be taken to pay them.

Partnership

EXPLANATION

A partnership is a group of between two and twenty people trading as one firm. They share responsibility for debts, decision making, and the profits.

ADVANTAGES

1. Again, you do not have to disclose the partnership's financial affairs to anyone other than the tax authorities.
2. It can be useful when partners have skills in different areas. For example, one person might be creative and another person organized.

DISADVANTAGES

All partners are personally liable for any business debts, even if they are caused by mismanagement by another partner. So it is essential to know your partners well, and trust them.

---

*See page 16 for more about invoices.
**See pages 24-25 for more about taxes.

Creating an office at home

You may be able to run a small business from your own home. You will need a table, a chair, drawers in which to store files, and a telephone. Before deciding, run through this checklist:

★ Does the contract or lease of my house forbid me to run a business from it?
★ Do I need planning permission for a change of use of the premises? Will I have to pay more rates?
★ Do my family mind? Will I disturb them or my neighbours with late deliveries, visits from customers, etc?

Finding premises away from home

Again, you should ask yourself some important questions before deciding on premises:

★ Shall I rent or buy? (It is usually better to rent premises until the business is well established.)

★ Can I make do with cheaper accommodation which is not centrally located?
★ Can I sell my goods from a market stall, which is both cheap to rent and convenient for customers?

Limited company (Ltd.)

EXPLANATION

A company formed by two or more shareholders who put money into the business in return for a share of the profits. They appoint directors who control the company. A limited company must be registered. You can get help from a solicitor to do this, or you can buy one which is already registered but is not trading.

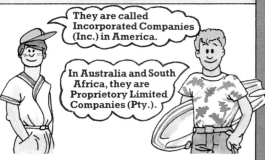

They are called Incorporated Companies (Inc.) in America.

In Australia and South Africa, they are Proprietory Limited Companies (Pty.).

ADVANTAGES

The financial liability of the shareholders is limited. If the business goes bust*, the personal belongings of the shareholders cannot be taken to pay the debts. You each lose only the value of the shares you own.

DISADVANTAGES

1. You may find it difficult to get credit from suppliers or loans from banks unless you give personal guarantees that you will pay your debts to them. This, though, places you in almost the same position as a sole trader or partnership.

2. In addition to sending details of your financial affairs to the taxman, you must send a copy of your annual accounts to the Registrar of Companies. These accounts must be checked by an outside accountant to prove that they present a true picture of the company's finances.

*See pages 36-37.

13

Selling

One of the most exciting parts of building up a business is when you begin to receive orders for your goods or services. The selling process is hard work, but also extremely satisfying. Some of the ways you can sell your goods or services are described below.

Direct selling

This is when you sell a product direct to the public, e.g. in your shop, market stall, or by mail order. Its great advantage is that by listening to comments made by customers, you can judge the market more accurately. It also means that you keep the profit normally taken by a middle man.

However, if you are making the product yourself it is time-consuming to stop working to deal with customers. You may also have to spend money on publicity (see right), especially if your premises are off the beaten track.

Mail order

You could advertise in newspapers or magazines, inviting customers to order goods from you by post. This is called mail order. Customers send in money with their orders. You may need to give a bank reference to the advertising department of the newspaper and they may also ask to see a sample of your work.

Direct mail

Direct mail is another way of selling by post. You send sales leaflets with order forms to potential customers. This can be uneconomical because the response rate is often low and may not be worth the cost of the leaflets and postage.

Working to order

If you provide a service or make personalized goods, you need to encourage orders from customers. Although many may come as a result of recommendations from satisfied customers, you must place yourself firmly in the public eye by promoting yourself.

How to promote yourself

★ Print leaflets, giving information about yourself and your work. You can deliver these to local houses, or ask friends to put them up on school or work noticeboards.

★ Write to magazines and local papers with interesting information about your work. Journalists are often looking for topics for their articles.

Look in the advertising section of newspapers and magazines for ideas on how to design an advertisement. Then try to draw one up for your business.

Selling to shops

If you sell your goods to retailers, you have to spend time calling in to shops with samples as you try to win orders. At first, you may feel that this is taking up too much of your production time and that your work is suffering. However, when you have established some satisfied buyers who place regular orders with you, the time you have to spend on selling will be less.

On the right, there are some tips on how to sell to shops.

★ Advertise in newspapers, specialist magazines, or on the local radio station. Remember to include a telephone number or address where you can be contacted. Budget for repeating your advertisement several times as a single one is rarely effective.

★ Create and keep a professional image. You should give the impression of confidence, and, above all, never be late for an appointment.

Well-designed letterheading is essential, and any packaging should give a feeling of quality.

If possible, make an appointment to see the manager or chief buyer.* Find out the name of the person you are going to see beforehand by asking another member of staff (e.g. the switchboard operator when you telephone).

Prepare what you are going to say and show; remember that shopkeepers are busy people, so be concise. Mention any aspects which might influence the shopkeeper in your favour – quality of materials, quick deliveries, etc.

Listen to the shopkeepers' reservations and see if your product can be adapted to suit their needs. Think about offering discounts for large orders or prompt payment, and help small shops by making eye-catching displays for your goods.

Customer files

Make a card index with the names and addresses of all your customers and potential customers, with comments about their particular needs and preferences. Remember to keep it up to date.

15

*You can find out about the role of a buyer on page 27.

Keeping the books

It is necessary to keep records of the financial affairs of even the smallest business. There are three main reasons for this. Firstly, they will remind you to pay your bills and collect your debts from customers on time. Secondly, you can see how much money you are making (or losing). Finally, they will enable you to work out how much tax you should pay.

You can find out how to keep accurate, clear accounts on these two pages.

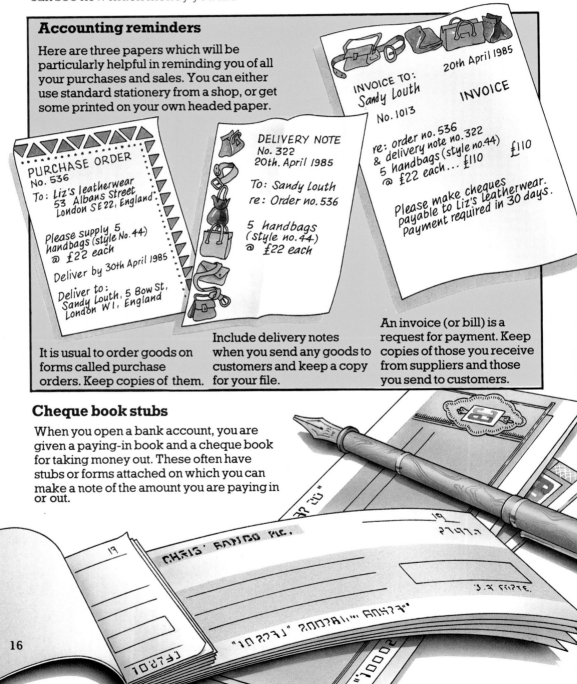

Accounting reminders

Here are three papers which will be particularly helpful in reminding you of all your purchases and sales. You can either use standard stationery from a shop, or get some printed on your own headed paper.

PURCHASE ORDER
No. 536
To: Liz's leatherwear
53 Albans Street
London SE22, England

Please supply 5
handbags (style No. 44)
@ £22 each

Deliver by 30th April 1985

Deliver to:
Sandy Louth, 5 Bow St,
London W1, England

DELIVERY NOTE
No. 322
20th. April 1985

To: Sandy Louth
re: Order no. 536

5 handbags
(style no. 44)
@ £22 each

INVOICE TO:
Sandy Louth   20th April 1985

No. 1013   INVOICE

re: order no. 536
& delivery note no. 322
5 handbags (style no.44)
@ £22 each... £110   £110

Please make cheques
payable to Liz's leatherwear.
Payment required in 30 days.

It is usual to order goods on forms called purchase orders. Keep copies of them.

Include delivery notes when you send any goods to customers and keep a copy for your file.

An invoice (or bill) is a request for payment. Keep copies of those you receive from suppliers and those you send to customers.

Cheque book stubs

When you open a bank account, you are given a paying-in book and a cheque book for taking money out. These often have stubs or forms attached on which you can make a note of the amount you are paying in or out.

Keeping records

It is useful to keep a record book of money put into the business and money taken out, entering each bill as it is paid. For a very simple system, all you need is a loose leaf binder and two sets of sheets, one for expenditure and one for sales. Every month or so, you should total up the money which has come in to the business and what has gone out.

Profit and loss

Using the information from these record sheets, you can draw up a profit and loss chart.

A profit and loss chart enables you to work out how much profit you have made during a given period. There are two things to take into consideration on top of the amount of sales and expenditure.

1. The cost of unsold goods you had at the start of the period (this is called opening stock), and of those you have at the time of drawing the chart (closing stock).

2. The decreased value of your equipment (this is called depreciation).

What is depreciation?

Say you were running a furniture removal service. For 10,000 tokens you buy a new van which you estimate will last you about five years. To spread the cost of this large sum over five years, you could "write off" 2,000 tokens from your accounts each year. This represents the decrease in value, or depreciation, of the van. If you want to replace the van in five years' time, you could open a savings account and put in 2,000 tokens each year from your profits.

Profit and loss from 1st Jan to 31st March	
IN	
Sales	100
OUT	
Expenditure	80
Depreciation	2
Opening stock	8
Less closing stock	(10)
	80
Profit	20

Dupont's restaurant

From the information here, can you draw up a profit and loss chart for Monsieur Dupont?

At the beginning of the month, Monsieur Dupont's opening stock is worth 80 francs.

He spends 800 francs on food, wine, overheads and so on. The monthly takings total 1,500 francs.

His closing stock is worth 100 francs. This month's contribution towards equipment etc. is 20 francs.

17

Growing bigger

Your business is doing well and you are thinking about expanding it. But take care; many small businesses make the mistake of growing too fast or in the wrong way. Before you make a firm decision to expand you should be confident that you can find new customers, products, premises, staff, and, most important of all, more money. Some of the problems you may be faced with are described below, and you will also find some suggestions on how to raise more money.

Finding more customers

This may not be easy. For example, if you have a shop, there is a limit to the distance that customers will travel. If you are providing a service, the time and cost of travelling to areas further afield could cut heavily into your profits.

Thinking up new ideas

This involves spending both time and money on researching the market and developing the new products or services to make sure that they meet the customers' requirements (see pages 20-21).

Training extra staff

Depending on your sort of business, you may have to train new staff.

Finding bigger premises

Expanding the premises of a small retail business could mean creating extra floor space by buying the shop next door, for example. Alternatively, you could buy a shop some distance away, but since you cannot be in two places at once, you will need reliable staff.

In a manufacturing business, expansion may mean building an extension to the premises or moving to bigger premises. Bear in mind the disruption to production when moving equipment.

Raising more money

All of the things described above cost money, and you should make sure that you can finance the growth of your business from the start.

Chris, for example, is running a picture framing business. He wants to expand his business by 50 per cent.

He first writes himself a chart called a balance sheet. A balance sheet gives you an instant assessment of where your money is in the business on any particular day – a sort of financial snapshot.

A balance sheet is divided up into assets (what the business owns) and liabilities (what the business owes).

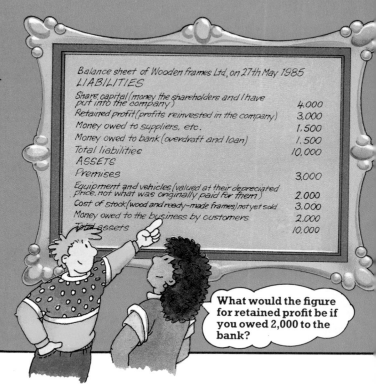

Balance sheet of Wooden frames Ltd, on 27th May 1985

LIABILITIES	
Share capital (money the shareholders and I have put into the company)	4,000
Retained profit (profits reinvested in the company)	3,000
Money owed to suppliers, etc.	1,500
Money owed to bank (overdraft and loan)	1,500
Total liabilities	10,000
ASSETS	
Premises	3,000
Equipment and vehicles (valued at their depreciated price, not what was originally paid for them)	2,000
Cost of stock (wood and ready-made frames) not yet sold	3,000
Money owed to the business by customers	2,000
Total assets	10,000

> What would the figure for retained profit be if you owed 2,000 to the bank?

The advantages of growing bigger

★ It is easier for a big business to get credit from suppliers or to raise loans from banks.

★ It is often cheaper to produce and sell in larger quantities because some costs (such as advertising) may stay the same, but can be spread over more goods. This is called economy of scale.

★ When a big business gets into financial trouble it may be able to turn to the government for help. Governments sometimes offer subsidies or loans to avoid problems such as regional unemployment.

Where can Chris get this money from?

Chris's total assets are 10,000 and his share capital, creditors, and overdraft only total 7,000. A balance sheet always balances, that is, the liabilities equal the assets. So the shareholders have a retained profit of 3,000. This is known as the "balancing figure".

From this chart, Chris can see how much money he will need to expand his business by 50 per cent.

Money needed to expand by 50 per cent

Extra premises:	1,500
Extra equipment:	1,000
Extra stock:	1,500
Extra debtors:	1,000
	5,000

Chris can safely increase the money he owes the bank and his creditors by 50 per cent. This gives him 1,500, but he still needs another 3,500. Below are some suggestions for where he can raise this money.

> He could rent the extra premises and hire or lease the extra equipment rather than buying them. Alternatively, he could sell his present premises and rent them back.

> He could ask his shareholders to put in the extra money, thus increasing the share capital. But they may not be prepared to, or may not have the money.

> He could wait until the business has made that money in extra profit; but this could take several years.

19

Expanding sales

As your business grows, it is necessary to rethink your sales plan so that you can encourage and cope with increased demand. You can find out some ways of doing this on these two pages.

Mail order

To expand your mail order business, it may be a good idea to identify the sort of customers who buy most of your goods and then try "target mailing". This means sending out sales literature to lots of people who are likely to be interested in a product. It is possible to buy lists of names and addresses of particular groups of people (for example, women aged 35-40 in the middle income bracket) from advertising agencies.

Another way of selling by mail order is to persuade magazines to run a special offer from your range of goods. You sell your product to the magazine at a discount (say 30 per cent) and the magazine then adds a small sum to cover the cost of the page involved, and the cost of sending out the goods. It then offers it to the reader for a sum less than the shop price. You may even be able to persuade the magazine to include your catalogue when sending off each order.

Direct selling

If you have your own retail outlet, such as a market stall or shop, you may decide to grow by increasing the size of the outlet or by buying or renting another outlet. Alternatively, you can rent space in a department store, employing your own sales staff. Many department stores now offer this "shop-within-a-shop" scheme because it allows them to employ fewer staff and have less money tied up in goods.

Selling through agents and sales reps

If you have been selling to shops, or some other retail outlet, you will probably not have time to go round more outlets to sell your goods. You may need to employ sales representatives (reps) or agents.

Agents are people who have a number of contacts and a specialist knowledge in a particular field. They work freelance for several clients at once. They make their money by taking a percentage (say ten per cent) on everything they sell.

It is possible to employ sales reps who work for you alone. The main advantage of this is that you can organize regular sales meetings, say once a month, where they can discuss with you and other members of your staff any suggestions or problems they have come across. They could also provide you with weekly sales reports giving any comments that customers have made about each product.

You have to pay their expenses, and may need to provide them with company cars.

Working to order

To increase the amount of work you do to order, it might be a good idea to try to attract customers with more money to spend. For example, you may have a catering business, where you do cooking for private parties. If you wrote to various companies, explaining the range of cooking you could offer, with some sample menus, you could obtain some really big orders such as regular Board Room lunches.

Price cutting

One way to attract customers from your competitors is to lower your prices. It is important to do your sums carefully to ensure that the increased sales will be enough to cover the loss in profit. Below you can see what happens to your costs and profit when you cut your prices.

Of course, if your sales go up considerably, your overheads may increase and you may have to take on extra staff. Also, your competitors may lower their prices to try and attract customers back, so your sales will drop. It is important to be aware of all these factors before you make any decisions.

Sales go up.

Overheads, own wages and labour costs stay the same.

Total material costs go up because more tea is sold.

Profit?

Price goes down.

Try it yourself

On page 42 there is a computer game which you can type into a home computer and play. You decide how much to charge customers for a cup of coffee and see what effect this has on your profit.

Points of law

On these two pages you can find out about some of the rights of a customer, of a tradesman, and of an employee. These people have differing interests in the world of business and so it is necessary to have laws to ensure that the rights of each are clearly defined. There is also some advice about insurance and the sort of disasters someone in business ought to insure against.

Customers' rights

Customers are entitled to expect goods to be fit for normal use. For example, a chair should withstand the weight of a normal human being.

Retailers must ensure that the goods on sale are free from defects, and must refund the money or offer to replace the goods if they are substandard. They can then take up the matter with their supplier if they wish.

Customers can expect a service to be done well, and can demand that the job is done again if it is done badly the first time. Ultimately, they can ask the culprit to pay for the cost of someone else putting the job right.

It is illegal to describe goods falsely either in advertisements, or verbally. Also, a trader cannot state that goods are reduced unless they have been at a higher price for a minimum period. (In the UK this is 28 days during the previous 12 months.)

Government watchdogs

Officers are employed by governments to check that laws are not being broken. They have the authority to enter shop premises and confiscate goods if necessary.

These officers can also check scales and other measuring devices such as petrol pumps. Traders might try to cheat customers by adjusting their scales to show a heavier weight.

Traders' rights

Traders may not challenge customers suspected of shop-lifting until they have removed the articles from the premises. They can then make a citizen's arrest and call the police who will take action if appropriate.

Any trader may insist that customers provide a banker's card if they wish to pay by cheque, to ensure that it is honoured by the bank.

If customers return goods which they have used, the retailer can refuse to refund the money or exchange the goods.

Employees' rights

In many countries, an employer must supply the employee with a contract of employment. The minimum amount of information you should put in it is listed on the right. These terms cannot then be altered without both parties' agreement. It is also illegal to discriminate against any employee because of colour, race or sex.

Name of employer and employee
Job-title
Starting date
Rate of pay (payable weekly or monthly)
Hours of work
Holidays and holiday pay
Sick pay
Pension scheme arrangements
Period of notice that should be given if employee wants to leave or employer wants to discharge employee.

Judge for yourself

Can you decide who is probably in the right in the following disputes?

Alan is at the cash till, about to pay for the goods in his trolley. However, the shopkeeper has seen him pocket some other items and challenges him. Can the police prosecute him?

Martin buys some climbing boots. Wearing them on his next climbing trip, he finds them very uncomfortable. Can he demand a refund at the shop he bought them from?

Suzie buys some yoghurt, but finds it is mouldy. The shopkeeper says that since she bought it before the sell-by date on the carton, she must complain to the manufacturer. Do you think this is true?

Insurance

Insurance allows you to take risks with less worry about what would happen if a disaster occurred.

The insurance company estimates the chances of an event happening, for example your premises catching fire. It then charges you a fee (called a premium) based on this estimate. In return, the insurance company guarantees to cover the cost of your loss.

It is possible to insure against almost any event, but the premiums may be so high that it is not worth your while. The picture on the left shows some hazards you might insure against.

23

Taxation

Many governments collect taxes from both private individuals and businesses to pay for schools, prisons and so on. Businesses have to pay various types of tax, some related to sales, some related to profit, some related to wages, and some related to local government (these are called rates). On these two pages you can find out about these various kinds of taxes.

Value Added Tax

In many countries a tax is added to the price of goods and services. In Britain this is called Value Added Tax (VAT). All businesses which have a high turnover*(in Britain, this is judged to be over about £20,000 per year) must register for VAT.

This means that you must add the tax on to the price of your goods or services, and pay this to the government about every three months. However, before doing so, you can deduct any VAT you have paid to your suppliers, so make sure you keep a record.

> How much VAT does Harry have to add to his bill for painting the room?

> Can you work out how much VAT Sue has to pay to the government per tin of paint?

A large manufacturing company produces paints. They charge retailers £10 per can, and add on VAT of 15%, making a total price of £11.50.

Harry is a decorator. He charges his customers £10 per hour for his time, plus the cost of the paint, which he buys from Sue. It takes him six hours to decorate one room, and two cans of paint.

Sue runs a home decorating shop. She buys the paint at £11.50 and sells it at £15 + 15% VAT = £17.25.

Sales tax

In some countries, such as the USA, there is a sales tax instead of VAT. The difference is that sales tax is only put on at the final stage, when the shop sells goods to the general public. Unlike VAT, sales tax is not usually added to services.

It is a much simpler system than VAT, but it does make it easier for people to slip through the system without paying sales tax. Dishonest people may claim that they are going to sell goods which they in fact keep.

24

*Turnover is the total income from sales during a period.

Income tax

In many countries, people are charged income tax on the money they earn. They pay a percentage of their annual income. Often it is the responsibility of the employer to deduct this from their pay and pass it on to the government. The employer must always keep a record of the amounts earned by each employee and the amount of tax that has been deducted.

Business tax

All businesses have to pay tax on their profits. How much tax you have to pay will be calculated according to your total income from sales minus your business expenses. This is why it is so important to keep accurate records of your expenditure (see pages 16-17).

National insurance

This is another kind of tax which employees in many countries have to pay as well as income tax. It goes partly towards financing state pensions (a payment made to retired people above a certain age) and social security, and partly into general taxation funds.

Building rates

In many countries, people who own premises have to pay a tax on them, called rates. The amount they have to pay is assessed according to the building's value, what sort of facilities it has, and so on.

A shop in the High Street is liable for much higher rates than the same size shop elsewhere.

If you operate a business from home, you may have to pay more rates than if you were just living there.

How can computers help in business?

Computers can be a great help in the routine tasks of a business. You can buy programs to do the following things:

★ Keep a record of each customer's account, calculating how much each owes and showing overdue bills.
★ Keep a record of VAT charged to customers and paid to suppliers.
★ Give up-to-the-minute balance sheets, cash flow charts, and profit and loss charts.
★ Analyze sales figures to show any significant trends in the market.
★ Print out routine reminders to customers about paying their bills, or mail shots telling them about a new service.

Protecting your ideas

You may have spent a great deal of time and money developing a wonderful new invention, and then the moment you put it on the market, someone copies you and steals half your customers. Two ways of making this illegal are described below and you can also find out about charging people money for copying your ideas.

Copyrighting

Many things can be protected by copyright including computer software, dress designs, books, artwork, and even design drawings and plans for manufactured goods. You can claim copyright by marking your work with the symbol ©, your name, and the year you completed it.

Patenting

You can patent an invention. This forbids anyone else from making and selling anything which uses your idea. However, it is necessary to apply for a patent and it can take up to two years to be processed. So make sure you put in your application well before you plan to sell your product.

Franchising

You can charge people money for selling goods identical to yours by granting them a franchise, or licence, in return for a percentage of their profits.* In this way, you can increase your sales without having to find extra finance.

Alternatively, you may wish to obtain a licence from others. The main advantage of this is that you start with a better knowledge of the costs, probable sales, and profits because you have the benefit of their experience.

The story of McDonald's

In 1937, Ray Kroc started a small business dealing in multimixers: machines which made lots of milkshakes at once. He found that a small restaurant in California, run by Mac and Dick McDonald, bought more multimixers than anyone else.

Despite the popularity of their hamburgers and milkshakes, the brothers did not want to expand. So in 1954 Kroc bought a licence from them to open restaurants like theirs anywhere in the USA in exchange for half a per cent of his sales income.

In 1961 he decided to buy the name McDonald outright for $2.7m. By the mid 1970s there were restaurants all over the world and the chain's annual sales are now over ten billion dollars a year. McDonald's serve about 18 million customers a day.

26

*This is normally about 6%.

Stock control

Although it is important that businesses do not run out of vital materials, it is also expensive to hold stock which is not needed. A company should operate with as little as possible. It is therefore necessary to have an efficient stock control system to tell you when you need to order new materials.

1. Two-bin method

You have two containers for each item which you keep in the stores. When the first bin is emptied, you order enough to fill it knowing that the amount in the second bin will keep you going until new supplies arrive. Of course, it is important to calculate the size of bin needed for each item.

2. Written records

This involves keeping records to show when deliveries arrive, how much is used of each item, and what the stock levels are at any given time. You can order just enough to ensure that you never run out. Nowadays this is often done by computers. You can even buy programs which automatically produce a purchase order when stocks fall to a minimum level.

You do have to store certain products. Whisky takes about ten years to mature.

Purchasers and buyers

Large companies often employ people who are responsible for negotiating with suppliers. In manufacturing business they are called purchasers, and in shops they are called buyers, but their job is much the same. They may also be in charge of stock control.

Buyers from large shops can lay down standards which must be met by their manufacturers. This not only applies to finished goods, but also to what goes into them.

Food, for example, must be made from the right quality of ingredients in the proportions specified by the retailer.

Buyers will visit each supplier to make sure that products are being made under hygienic conditions.

Exporting

Once you have exploited the market in your home country as far as possible, you may decide to explore markets further afield. This can be very expensive to begin with, however, and you should be certain that your business will be able to stand the initial investment of both time and money.

On these two pages you can find out about exporting and there is also some advice on things to think about before you decide to take your product to foreign lands.

Researching overseas markets

Each country has different needs and expectations, and so you will have to conduct market research on each one separately. You should visit each country and look carefully into the possibilities it offers. You may find that you have to redesign and adapt your products accordingly.

Here are some factors to consider when choosing a market.

1. The potential of your product there. Will the customer want or need it? For example, your beautiful rainwear will probably be left on the shelf in Saudi Arabia.

2. The cost of exporting your goods, including transport, distribution, import taxes, legal requirements and so on. You can then work out a new minimum price which you should charge for your product and compare it with competitors' to see if it is realistic.

3. The competition. Your product should be significantly better than other products already on the market otherwise you will find it difficult to sell to foreign customers.

Selling your products abroad

There are five main channels of exporting. The one you choose will depend to some extent on your product, and also on how much time you have to spend on exporting.

1. Through overseas buyers

Many overseas firms have buyers based in different countries who are looking for goods to import. You can find out the names and addresses of buyers who are interested in your type of product through government bodies.

2. Through an export house

An export house will secure foreign orders for you. In return for a commission, they will take care of the packing, transportation, insurance and finance necessary to export your goods, and they will organize payment for your goods. However, it does mean that you lose all control over the marketing of your goods.

Drawing up a contract

When drawing up a contract with a customer, you must agree the date of payment, how the money will be paid, and in which currency. In these matters, your bank will be a great help, and it may make tactful enquiries for you about your customers through its international links.

You should also agree on the amount of responsibility each of you will take in delivering the goods. This includes not only transportation, but also the cost of insuring the goods from the moment they leave your building to their arrival at their destination.

Government help

Governments often encourage businesses to export goods as it brings more money into the country. Because of this, there are numerous government organizations available to give advice to exporters. For example, there may be a computerized service which will pinpoint market opportunities for your product and you may be eligible for cheap loans or special grants. You can find out more about these organizations from your local library.

Embassies of the country to which you are planning to export can also be invaluable. They will provide specific information such as names and addresses of outlets and companies in their country that might be interested in your product.

3. Employing overseas agents

You can employ foreign sales agents to get orders for your goods from customers in their own country.

4. Selling directly from home

If you deal directly from your own country, it is important that you keep in close contact with foreign customers to ensure that your product is not overlooked. You should also be aware of any changes in the market. This will take up quite a lot of your time.

5. Selling from an overseas sales base

When you are planning to trade a great deal in a particular country it is often a good idea to establish a sales base there. The staff can then be responsible for the entire marketing of the product.

Marketing

As a business grows, it may diversify into different products, or lines. A big business may have such a wide range of products that a whole marketing department is dedicated to monitoring sales and developing new lines. The diagram below shows what happens before any new product is put on to the shop shelves.

Where do ideas originate?

Marketing teams get ideas for new products from four main sources:

1. Competitors' lines

This is the "me too" source. If a rival company brings out a particular line which does well, the marketing team will explore the possibility of bringing out a similar line to ensure they have a share of the market.

2. Brainstorming

Colleagues, customers, friends and so on are encouraged to make suggestions. Most of the ideas they come up with are impractical, but sometimes a winner turns up.

3. Gaps in the market

The marketing team will be continually looking out for new opportunities. For example, a craze for a new sport will bring opportunities for sportswear and equipment.

4. Overseas products

A member of the marketing team will be responsible for keeping an eye out for products abroad which might be suitable for the home market.

1 Idea: Luxury diet coleslaw

Define the product

4

The marketing people now instruct artists to work on designs for the packaging of the product. They also inform an advertising agency about the product, letting it know the market they are aiming at, what image they are trying to present, what competition there is and why this product is better, and a rough price for it. This gives the advertisers time to prepare campaigns informing the public about the new product.

Is the price realistic?

5

The research and development team can now come up with samples and rough costs and the marketing people estimate how many they can sell in a five year, three year or one year period. They then calculate a shelf price for the product taking into account their company's profit and the retailer's mark-up. After comparing this with their competitors' prices they can see whether it is realistic.
If no: revise. If yes: carry on.

② Can it be made?

A special department called the research and development department will find out whether the product can be made.

If the answer is no, revise the proposal.

If the answer is yes, carry on.

③ Does the customer want it?

Members of the marketing department will tell a market research agency about their idea, specifying the sort of person they are aiming at. The market researchers then produce a questionnaire which they ask a selected number of people to answer. From this they can gauge the amount of interest there is in the idea, and what sort of demand there may be for it. They will find out information such as how much customers may be prepared to pay for it, and what sort of packaging they prefer.

If the answer is no, revise (they may be aiming at the wrong sort of people) or scrub.

If the answer is yes, carry on.

⑥ Does it live up to expectations?

The market research agency presents a group of people in the same category as the first group with samples of the actual product. They may have liked the idea of the product – but do they like the actual thing? Will they still want to buy it?

If no: can the product be modified? If not, scrub the proposal. If it can, go back to Does the customer want it?

If yes: carry on.

⑦ Proceed to launch

The marketing department then arranges for the production team to make the right number of tubs of coleslaw to fit in with their sales forecast.

The marketing people inform sales reps about the product and the market it is aimed at. They decide on any promotional material they would like to support it in the shops, such as free offers, competitions, and so on.

⑧ Launch

The sales reps sell the new product to retailers, and the marketing team ensures that it is delivered to them at the right time.

Going public

A business can raise enormous sums of money by selling shares in the company to members of the public. This is called going public. When people buy shares they become part-owners in the company. Potential shareholders must be confident that the value of shares they buy will not go down. This means that most public companies are well established.

After first being issued, the shares are bought and sold on a special market called the Stock Market, or Stock Exchange. Although the price of each share sold on the Stock Market may change every day, this does not normally affect the company.

How does a company go public?

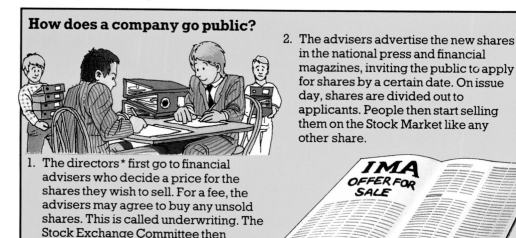

2. The advisers advertise the new shares in the national press and financial magazines, inviting the public to apply for shares by a certain date. On issue day, shares are divided out to applicants. People then start selling them on the Stock Market like any other share.

1. The directors* first go to financial advisers who decide a price for the shares they wish to sell. For a fee, the advisers may agree to buy any unsold shares. This is called underwriting. The Stock Exchange Committee then examines the company thoroughly to check that it is financially sound.

The London Stock Exchange

There are Stock Exchanges in many major cities including New York, Tokyo, Hong Kong, Melbourne and Paris. One of the biggest and most famous is the London Stock Exchange. There are two types of people who are involved in the actual deals on the floor of the London Stock Exchange. 1. Brokers. These are agents through whom members of the public buy and sell shares. They have a knowledge of the market and can advise their clients. They charge clients a commission based on the value of each transaction. 2. Jobbers. These are like stallholders in a street market, but they deal in shares. Their profit comes from the difference between their buying and selling price; this is known as the jobber's turn. A jobber alters the price of each share according to the demand for it. Only the London Stock Exchange uses jobbers; elsewhere brokers have to find both buyers and sellers for shares.

32

*See page 13.

What do you get if you buy a share?

1 Any increase in the value of the share. If the price goes down, though, you lose. You can sell at any time.

2 Dividends. These are a proportion of the business' profits paid out once or twice a year to the shareholders. However, if the company is doing badly, the directors may decide not to pay out dividends.

3 You can attend and vote at shareholders' meetings where policy decisions are made.

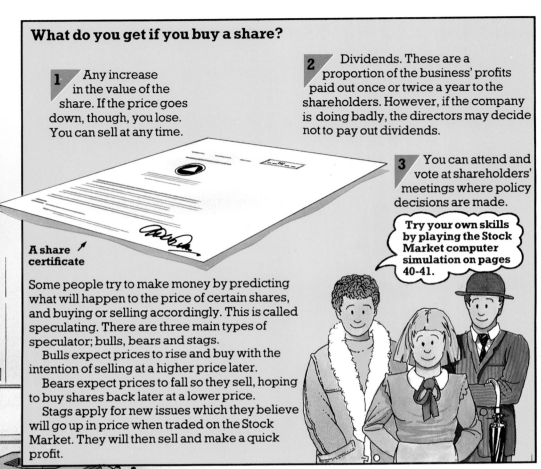

A share certificate

Try your own skills by playing the Stock Market computer simulation on pages 40-41.

Some people try to make money by predicting what will happen to the price of certain shares, and buying or selling accordingly. This is called speculating. There are three main types of speculator; bulls, bears and stags.

Bulls expect prices to rise and buy with the intention of selling at a higher price later.

Bears expect prices to fall so they sell, hoping to buy shares back later at a lower price.

Stags apply for new issues which they believe will go up in price when traded on the Stock Market. They will then sell and make a quick profit.

How do jobbers and brokers make a deal?

1. Judy wishes to sell her 500 shares. She asks a broker to sell them for her. On the Stock Exchange floor, the broker goes to a jobber who deals in these shares and asks him to name his prices for the shares. He does not reveal whether he wishes to buy or sell at this stage because the jobber could then increase or decrease the prices to his own advantage. 2. The jobber quotes his buying price and his selling price. The broker then goes on to some more jobbers, trying to find the highest price. Having found the jobber with the best price, the broker says, "I'll sell you 500 at 143". 3. The deal has now been made, as the motto of the Stock Exchange is "My word is my bond". Both jobber and broker make a note of the deal in their "bargain books". On settlement day (which occurs about every two weeks) the jobber pays the broker for the shares. Having deducted his commission and any tax that is liable, the broker sends the money to Judy.

Building a business empire

Some people are ambitious enough to want to build up a business empire. They are motivated by the great financial rewards, power and influence that it can bring. On these two pages you can find out about these empires and how they are built.

Expanding sideways

The company expands by doing the same activities as before, but on a larger scale. For example, an ice-cream manufacturer would produce more and more, eventually cornering a large share of the market.

Expanding upwards and downwards

This is when the company expands into other stages of production in the same industry. So the ice-cream manufacturer might take over the selling side of it too.

Diversifying

The company expands into completely different fields with which it has had no previous connection. So the ice-cream manufacturer might start producing sausages as well. The great advantage is that this keeps the staff occupied and brings money in during the decrease in demand for ice-cream during the winter.

Take-overs and mergers

One way of expanding a business rapidly is by take-over or merger. A take-over is when a company buys enough shares in another company to make it the major shareholder and therefore to have the largest vote. It can then take over the running of the company.

A merger is when two or more companies are joined together to form a new company. The shareholders of each company exchange their old shares for shares in the new company.

Which company?

When looking for companies to take over or merge with, you should obviously look for those which will particularly benefit your firm in some way, such as those shown below.

1. A major supplier or major sales outlet – this will ensure you get favourable treatment.
2. A company with a good share of the same market (this will reduce competition).
3. A company with a good technological advantage.

A company about to take over another is called the predator.

A company about to be taken over is called the target.

The shareholders' position

If there are not enough shares on the Stock Market available for a predator to buy, it will make a formal offer to the shareholders of either cash or some of its own shares. In either case, the offer will be higher than the market price, in order to persuade shareholders to sell.

Because the shareholders are in a powerful position, rumours of take-overs often cause the price of shares to rise. If the target company is against the take-over, there can be a long and bitter battle between the two companies, each trying to win the shareholders' support.

Monopolies

A company can grow so big that it is able to eliminate all its competitors and therefore have the market all to itself. This is called a monopoly. The word monopoly comes from the Greek words *monos* meaning only, and *poleein* meaning to sell.

A company could become a monopoly by lowering its prices for a short period thus putting competitors out of business if they are unable to do the same. Alternatively, it can give suppliers large orders so that they no longer have time to work for anyone else.

Anti-monopoly safeguards

Monopolies have a tremendous amount of power because they are the only producers of certain goods. This means that they are able to charge extortionate prices in the safe knowledge that customers cannot shop elsewhere. For this reason there are laws to protect customers against possible monopolies being formed.

International and multinational companies

Very large companies sell their goods all over the world. They can be either international or multinational.

International companies are firms that operate mostly from one country but export to other countries. For example, Toyota makes most of its cars in Japan but they are sold throughout the Western world.

Multinational companies have their headquarters in one country but have factories and offices elsewhere, which operate in many ways as independent companies. For example, General Motors is based in America but own Vauxhall in Britain, Opel in Germany and Holden in Australia. Important decisions are made in America, but the European managers make most of the decisions concerning their own companies without referring to the American headquarters.

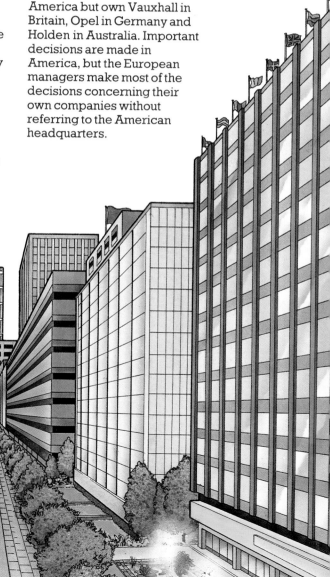

Going bust

Not all businesses become empires overnight. Some get into severe financial difficulties and cannot meet their debts. This is known as being insolvent. Below there is advice on noticing danger signals. You can also find out what happens when a sole trader or partnership goes bankrupt, or a company goes into liquidation.

Why do businesses go bust?

The main reason for the failure of most businesses is lack of control of cash flow. When you sell goods or services on credit you should make a profit, but if the customer takes a long time to pay, you could run out of money with which to pay your suppliers and employees.

How to control your cash flow

Just as locks control the flow of water in a canal, you can control your cash flow by taking a number of precautions.

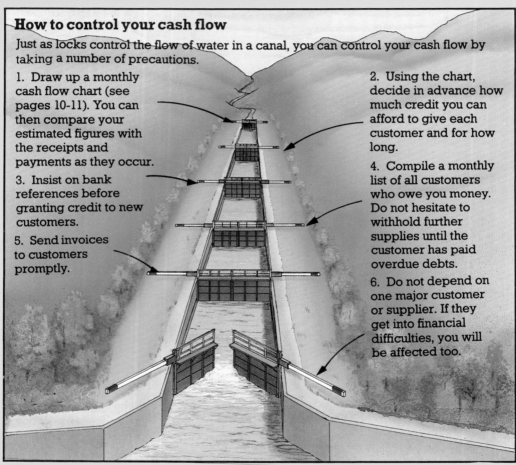

1. Draw up a monthly cash flow chart (see pages 10-11). You can then compare your estimated figures with the receipts and payments as they occur.

3. Insist on bank references before granting credit to new customers.

5. Send invoices to customers promptly.

2. Using the chart, decide in advance how much credit you can afford to give each customer and for how long.

4. Compile a monthly list of all customers who owe you money. Do not hesitate to withhold further supplies until the customer has paid overdue debts.

6. Do not depend on one major customer or supplier. If they get into financial difficulties, you will be affected too.

The bankruptcy procedure

If a sole trader or partnership cannot pay its debts, one or more of its major creditors can ask the courts for a bankruptcy order. The courts will then appoint a trustee who will take possession of the debtor's property. The trustee will ensure a fair distribution of the debtor's property to creditors; this may include stock, assets, equipment and personal possessions.

Having been declared bankrupt, you may not set up a business again unless you have been discharged by the courts. When you are discharged you are free to make a fresh start and your slate is wiped clean. The courts may discharge you after a set period of time, say five years, if you have managed to pay off a percentage of your debts in that time.

Record breaking bankruptcy

One of the biggest bankruptcy cases is that of William Stern. His company, the Willstar Group Holding Company, dealt in buying, developing and selling property. However, in the 1970s, the price of property fell, and Stern's company fell with it. In February 1983, his debts totalled £142,978,413. The courts agreed that he could be discharged in two and a half years' time if he paid £500,000 of his debts.

Liquidation

If a limited or public company builds up large debts it cannot pay, it goes into liquidation. This can either be voluntary or compulsory liquidation. If it is voluntary liquidation, the directors promise to pay all its debts within a certain period (12 months in the UK). However, if the company has not gone into voluntary liquidation, an unpaid creditor may apply to the courts for compulsory liquidation of the company. A liquidator, or receiver, is then appointed to look after the affairs of the company, paying its debts and sometimes winding it up.

In both cases, the directors must prepare a full statement of the company's affairs, listing its assets and liabilities, and why it is in debt. The company must also stop trading.

Directors of large companies sometimes give press conferences to explain the situation to the shareholders.

Priority on debts

If a business is liquidated, some people have a greater right than others to any money or assets belonging to the company. The order of priority is shown below.

Legal fees and liquidator's payment.

Preferential creditors. These include tax collectors and employees.

Secured creditors. These include banks.

Ordinary creditors. These may get very little or nothing.

Shareholders who, depending on the extent of the debts, may lose all the money they have invested in the company.

What to do if your business is going badly

If you have a temporary cash flow problem, there are a number of paths you may be able to follow without going bankrupt or into liquidation.

1. Raise some money from the bank. If the company that owes you money is secure, for example a large, prosperous company, a bank may be prepared to tide you over with a short-term loan.

2. Sell some assets, for example stock, or sell your premises and rent them back.

3. You may be able to sell the business at a low price.

Success stories

Vidal Sassoon

Vidal Sassoon was born in a very poor area in the East End of London. At the age of 14 he got a job at a hairdressers' in the East End of London. He learned the trade by washing and cutting the hair of local tramps; he paid them for the privilege.

Vidal progressed to becoming the manager of a hairdressing shop. Then, in 1959 he created a revolutionary hairstyle which rejected the fashion of back-combing and teasing women's hair. Named "The Shape", it was the first of many fascinating geometrical designs which made Vidal Sassoon famous worldwide.

From designing radical new haircuts, Vidal progressed in three different directions. Firstly, he promoted general health and good look and co-wrote the best-seller "Year of Beauty and Health".

Secondly, he introduced a complete line of hair care products under the Vidal Sassoon name. By 1977, these were being exported to markets all over the world. In May 1983, sales were over $110,000,000.

Thirdly, he set up numerous hairdressing schools, including the London Academy, which recently trained its millionth student.

Marks and Spencer

Michael Marks, a Lithuanian Jew, emigrated to England in about 1883 and arrived with no money, knowing no English, and unable to read or write. He set up in business in Leeds as a pedlar of buttons, pins, needles and so on, carrying goods from house to house on his back.

In 1884 he took a stall in Leeds market. Over the stall he hung a board saying "Don't ask the price, it's a penny", a slogan which proved to be very successful.

Michael then expanded by opening more stalls in nearby areas, and in 1891 he established a warehouse. He decided to take on an acquaintance, Tom Spencer, as a partner. They each had shares in the business worth £300.

In 1903 they registered Marks and Spencer as a limited company with themselves as the main shareholders. The company flourished. Soon there were over 50 branches selling a variety of goods.

Some were clothes shops, and this became the pattern for future expansion. However, in 1905 Tom died and in 1907 Michael also died leaving Tom's son, his executor (William Chapman), and his own son, Simon, in charge.

Laura Ashley

In 1953 Bernard and Laura Ashley started a business printing tablemats and scarves. They used silk screens on an old kitchen table in their small attic apartment in Pimlico, London. They sold their products to small shops and department stores in London. Cash flow was a problem as at the start they had only £10 to put into the business.

Overcrowding forced the production part of the business into a nearby basement where Bernard developed a larger, more efficient printing machine. They produced greater quantities and added furnishing and dress fabrics to their list.

The cost of property made further expansion in London impossible, so they moved to Surrey where they used an old coach shed as their factory. Bernard built an even larger printing machine, and the extra production enabled them to start exporting to foreign markets including France, Holland, the U.S. and Australia.

Increasing orders meant they had to expand the factory. Planning regulations forced them out of Surrey and into Wales where they were able to finance a new factory relatively cheaply. Inspired by the beautiful Welsh countryside, Laura designed two dresses which could be produced at a very low price.

Sales of the dresses were high, but the business could not cope with the credit which their customers expected. Laura and Bernard decided to go direct to the public by opening a shop in London. At first this was not a success. Then Bernard had the idea of advertising the £6 dresses on the underground, giving the shop as a stockist.

Customers poured in and their payments restored the cash flow problem. Profits were ploughed back into more factories, shops and research. Factories were opened in Holland, Ireland and America, with new warehouses in London, Paris and New Jersey. Today there are well over 200 shops all over the world.

In 1917 Chapman and Spencer retired from the board of directors due to a difference of opinion. Marks brought in his brother-in-law, Israel Sieff, to help him.

The company went from strength to strength and they became a public company in 1926. The Spencer family sold some of their shares which by then were worth over 500 times the original £300.

In the later 1940s, the company started a policy of only selling goods bearing their own label, that of St Michael. They improved links with suppliers so that they could control quality, and St Michael goods built up a solid reputation. Seeing that there would be a limit to their expansion in clothing, they diversified into food and homeware items which proved to be just as successful.

In addition to their reputation for quality and value for money, they also built up a reputation for staff welfare. They installed canteens and were amongst the first companies to offer medical and dental services to employees.

COMPUTER PROGRAMS

On the next few pages there are some programs which will work on the Commodore 64, Vic 20*, Apple, TRS-80 Colour Computer**, BBC, Electron, MSX and Spectrum. When you have typed them in, run each program and follow the instructions on the screen.

Some lines will need converting for the different computers and these are marked ★. The conversions are listed in the chart on page 43.

Coffee stall program

This program shows you the effect of price on sales and profit (see page 21). The lower the price, the more cups you will sell, but the lower your profit will be on each cup. See if you can find the price which will give you the biggest profit.

```
★  10  CLS
   20  LET NC=180:LET FC=1000
   30  PRINT "PRICE PER CUP":INPUT PC
   40  IF PC<0 THEN GOTO 30
   50  LET NC=NC-NC/20*(PC-10)
   60  IF NC<0 THEN LET NC=0
   70  IF NC>180 THEN LET FC=FC+100
   80  LET VC=5*NC
   90  LET SL=PC*NC
  100  LET PR=SL-(VC+FC)
  110  PRINT:PRINT "SALES....";NC;" CUPS"
  120  PRINT "PRICE....";PC;" UNITS"
  130  PRINT:PRINT "SALES INCOME.....";SL;" UNITS"
  140  PRINT "TOTAL MATERIAL COSTS.....";VC;" UNITS"
  150  PRINT "OVERHEADS AND OWN WAGES..";FC;" UNITS"
  160  LET P$="PROFIT"
  170  IF PR<0 THEN LET P$="LOSS"
  180  PRINT:PRINT P$;"....";ABS(PR);" UNITS "
```

Fashion shop program

This program gives you a chance to see how good you would be at running a chain of fashion clothes shops. You can make a number of policy decisions such as how much to spend on advertising, how many staff to employ, how many shops to run and how many goods to keep in stock.

You have a bank loan which you have to pay back in monthly instalments from your cash account. Be careful; if your cash account goes overdrawn more than two months running, you will go bust.

The characters beside the program listing will give you hints to help you make your decisions. You can also instruct the computer to draw up a balance sheet, company report, profit and loss account or cash flow analysis.

```
★  10  DIM F(6)
★  20  LET C$="£":LET CF=0
   30  LET LB=12000:LET M=2000:LET MO=0:LET NS=3:LET EM=10:LET AD=100
   40  LET SK=80000:LET E$="N":LET S$="N":LET S=20000:LET SL=3000
   50  LET MN=1:LET OW=SL+M+SK+S:LET FD=0:LET FF=0:LET SD=0
   60  DATA 5,3,40,5,150,8
   70  FOR K=1 TO 6:READ F(K)
   80  NEXT K
   90  LET MU=F(5):LET PR=F(1)
  100  LET SC=INT(SK/PR):LET DR=INT(MO/PR)
  110  GOSUB 1580
  120  PRINT:PRINT "OPTIONS: MONTH ";MN:PRINT
  130  PRINT "1.COMPANY REPORT":PRINT "2.BALANCE SHEET"
  140  PRINT "3.CASH FLOW ANALYSIS":PRINT "4.PROFIT/LOSS ACCOUNT"
  150  PRINT "5.NEXT MONTH":PRINT
  160  PRINT "ENTER NUMBER"
  170  INPUT N:LET N=INT(N):IF N<1 OR N>5 THEN GOTO 110
  180  IF MN=1 AND N>1 AND N<5 THEN PRINT "NOT AVAILABLE THIS MONTH":GOTO 160
★ 190  ON N GOSUB 210,1170,1340,1390,360
  200  GOTO 110
  210  GOSUB 1580:PRINT:PRINT "COMPANY REPORT:":PRINT
  220  PRINT "YOU HAVE ";NS;" SHOPS"
```

* Vic 20 needs a memory expansion   ** Extended BASIC version

```
230 LET X=ABS(M)
240 IF M>0 THEN PRINT "BANK BALANCE: ";:GOSUB 1600:PRINT
250 IF M<0 THEN PRINT "OVERDRAFT: ";:GOSUB 1600:PRINT " !!!!"
260 IF LB>0 THEN PRINT "BANK LOAN: ";:LET X=LB:GOSUB 1600:PRINT
270 PRINT "OWING FOR ORDERS: ";:LET X=MO:GOSUB 1600:PRINT
280 LET FF=1:PRINT "STOCK LEVEL: ";:LET X=SC:GOSUB 1620:PRINT " ITEMS"
290 PRINT "ON ORDER: ";:LET X=DR:GOSUB 1620:PRINT " ITEMS"
300 PRINT "ITEMS SOLD: ";:LET X=SD:GOSUB 1620:PRINT:LET FF=0
310 PRINT "CURRENT MARKUP: ";MU;" PERCENT"
320 PRINT "STAFF: ";EM
330 IF S$="Y" THEN PRINT "YOU HAVE REACHED MARKET SATURATION"
340 IF E$<>"N" THEN PRINT "YOU HAVE BEGUN EXPORTING"
350 GOSUB 1590:RETURN
360 GOSUB 1580:PRINT:PRINT "MANAGEMENT DIRECTIVE FOR MONTH ";MN:PRINT
370 PRINT "HOW MANY SHOPS DO YOU WANT TO OPERATE":INPUT AS
380 LET AS=INT(AS):IF AS<=0 THEN GOTO 1080
390 PRINT "HOW MANY STAFF WILL YOU EMPLOY":INPUT AM
400 LET AM=INT(AM):IF AM<AS THEN GOTO 390
410 PRINT "PERCENTAGE PROFIT MARKUP":INPUT MU
420 LET MU=INT(MU):IF MU<0 THEN GOTO 410
430 PRINT "MONEY TO SPEND ON ADVERTISING":INPUT AA
440 LET AA=INT(AA):IF AA<0 THEN LET AA=0
450 PRINT "NUMBER OF ITEMS TO BE ORDERED":INPUT AR
460 LET AR=INT(AR):IF AR<0 THEN GOTO 450
470 IF AR=0 THEN LET AO=0:GOTO 500
480 PRINT "COST PRICE PER ITEM":INPUT AO
490 LET AO=INT(AO):IF AR>0 AND AO<1 THEN GOTO 480
500 IF S$="Y" THEN PRINT "YOU HAVE REACHED MARKET SATURATION"
510 IF S$<>"Y" THEN GOTO 540
520 IF E$="N" THEN PRINT "DO YOU WISH TO START EXPORTING (Y/N)":GOSUB 1550
530 IF E$="N" AND A$="Y" THEN LET E$="Y"
540 LET MN=MN+1:LET OV=SL
550 IF AM<EM THEN LET EM=AM
560 LET MI=0:LET RL=0
570 IF AS>=NS THEN GOTO 600
580 LET MI=SL:LET SL=INT(SL*AS/NS)
590 LET MI=MI-SL:LET NS=AS:LET RL=MI
600 LET CS=(EM/NS)/F(2)
610 IF CS>1.5 THEN LET CS=1.5
620 LET CS=(3+CS)/4:LET CA=1600
630 IF CA>SC/NS THEN LET CA=SC/NS
640 LET CA=CA*NS
650 LET AD=INT(AA+(AD/4))
660 LET AF=AD*F(3)/100000:LET AF=(4+AF)/4
670 LET LF=SC*F(6)/20000:IF LF>2 THEN LET LF=2
680 LET LF=(5+LF)/6:LET QF=1:IF PR>F(1) THEN LET QF=1-(PR-F(1))/5.5
690 IF QF<0 THEN LET QF=0
700 LET VF=2-MU/F(5):IF VF<0 THEN LET VF=0
710 LET SD=INT(CA*0.2*CS*AF*LF*QF*VF)
720 IF E$="S" THEN LET ES=INT(5000*F(4)/(PR*10))
730 IF E$<>"S" THEN LET ES=0
740 LET SD=SD+ES:IF SD>=SC THEN LET SD=SC-1
750 IF SD<0 THEN LET SD=0
760 LET OS=SK:LET SC=SC-SD
770 LET SK=SK-INT(SD*PR)
780 LET SS=INT(SD*PR*(100+MU)/100)
790 LET SS=SS+INT(ES*PR*MU/200)
800 LET MI=MI+SS:LET SC=SC+DR
810 LET SK=SK+MO:LET PR=SK/SC:LET MT=MO
820 LET MO=AO*AR:LET DR=AR:LET CB=0
830 IF AS<=NS THEN GOTO 870
```

If you don't have enough staff, you won't sell many goods. But new staff cost a lot to train, so don't go overboard!

The price you pay your suppliers for stock will affect the price you can charge, and how many you sell. But very cheap clothes are bad quality and will not sell well.

```
840 LET CB=((AS-NS)*10000)
850 LET MT=MT+CB:LET SL=SL+((AS-NS)*2000)
860 LET NS=AS
870 IF NS<6 THEN LET S$="N"
880 IF NS>=6 THEN LET S$="Y"
890 LET MT=MT+(NS*500):LET DP=INT(SL/4)
900 LET EC=0
910 IF E$="S" THEN LET EC=3000
920 IF E$="Y" THEN LET EC=15000:LET E$="S"
930 LET MT=MT+EC
940 LET SL=SL-DP:IF AM<=EM THEN GOTO 960
950 LET MT=MT+((AM-EM)*50):LET EM=AM
960 LET MT=MT+(EM*600)+AA
970 LET IL=0:LET LP=0
980 IF LB>0 THEN LET IL=INT(0.01*LB):LET LP=INT(0.01*12000)
990 LET IM=M:LET M=M+MI-MT
1000 LET IM=INT(0.005*(M+IM)/2)
1010 IF IM<=0 THEN LET IM=IM*2
1020 LET M=M+IM-(LP+IL):LET LB=LB-LP
1030 LET MT=MT+LP+IL-IM+200:LET EX=MT
1040 LET PL=MI+SL+SK-MT-OS-OV
1050 IF M<0 THEN LET FD=FD+1
1060 IF M>0 THEN LET FD=0
1070 IF FD<2 OR M>0 THEN RETURN
1080 GOSUB 1580:PRINT
1090 IF M<0 THEN PRINT "YOU HAVE GONE BUST!":PRINT
1100 LET NW=SL+M+SK+S
1110 PRINT "VALUE OF BUSINESS AT START ";:LET X=OW:GOSUB 1600:PRINT
1120 PRINT "VALUE OF BUSINESS AT WINDUP ";:LET X=NW:GOSUB 1600:PRINT:PRINT
1130 LET CH=NW-OW:LET X=ABS(CH)
1140 IF CH>=0 THEN PRINT "SHOWING PROFIT OF ";:GOSUB 1600:PRINT
1150 IF CH<0 THEN PRINT "SHOWING LOSS OF ";:GOSUB 1600:PRINT
1160 STOP
1170 GOSUB 1580:PRINT:PRINT "BALANCE SHEET:"
1180 PRINT:PRINT "-LIABILITIES-"
1190 PRINT "SHARE CAPITAL ";:LET X=S:GOSUB 1600:PRINT
1200 LET AX=SL+SK:LET LI=MO+S+LB
1210 IF M<0 THEN LET LI=LI-M
1220 IF M>0 THEN LET AX=AX+M
1230 PRINT "RETAINED PROFIT ";:LET X=AX-LI:GOSUB 1600:PRINT
1240 PRINT "MONEY OWED TO SUPPLIERS ";:LET X=MO:GOSUB 1600:PRINT
1250 IF LB>0 THEN PRINT "BANK LOAN ";:LET X=LB:GOSUB 1600:PRINT
1260 IF M<0 THEN PRINT "OVERDRAFT ";:LET X=ABS(M):GOSUB 1600:PRINT
1270 PRINT "TOTAL LIABILITIES = ";:LET X=AX:GOSUB 1600:PRINT
1280 PRINT:PRINT "-ASSETS-"
1290 PRINT "EQUIPMENT ";:LET X=SL:GOSUB 1600:PRINT
1300 PRINT "STOCK NOT SOLD ";:LET X=SK:GOSUB 1600:PRINT
1310 IF M>0 THEN PRINT "BANK BALANCE ";:LET X=M:GOSUB 1600:PRINT
1320 PRINT "TOTAL ASSETS = ";:LET X=AX:GOSUB 1600:PRINT
1330 GOSUB 1590:RETURN
1340 GOSUB 1580:PRINT:PRINT "CASH FLOW:":PRINT
1350 PRINT "MONEY IN ";:LET X=MI:GOSUB 1600:PRINT
1360 PRINT "MONEY OUT ";:LET X=MT:GOSUB 1600:PRINT
1370 PRINT:PRINT "DIFFERENCE BETWEEN":PRINT "MONEY IN AND MONEY OUT ";
1380 LET X=MI-MT:GOSUB 1600:PRINT:GOSUB 1590:RETURN
1390 GOSUB 1580:PRINT:PRINT "PROFIT AND LOSS ACCOUNT:"
1400 PRINT:PRINT "-IN-"
1410 PRINT "SALES ";:LET X=SS:GOSUB 1600:PRINT
1420 IF RL>0 THEN PRINT "SALE OF SHOPS ";:LET X=RL:GOSUB 1600:PRINT
1430 PRINT:PRINT "-OUT-"
1440 PRINT "EXPENDITURE (OVERHEADS, STOCK, STAFF, OWN WAGES, BANK) ";
1450 LET X=EX-CB-EC:GOSUB 1600:PRINT
```

It costs a lot to set up a shop, so think carefully before expanding. However, the secondhand value of fixtures and fittings is minimal, so don't be too ready to sell shops, either.

Remember, unless you advertise regularly for a few months, the effect will be minimal.

```
1460 IF EC>0 THEN PRINT "EXPORT COSTS ";:LET X=EC:GOSUB 1600:PRINT
1470 IF CB>0 THEN PRINT "SETTING UP NEW SHOPS ";:LET X=CB:GOSUB 1600:PRINT
1480 PRINT "DEPRECIATION OF ASSETS ";:LET X=DP:GOSUB 1600:PRINT
1490 PRINT "OPENING STOCK ";:LET X=OS:GOSUB 1600:PRINT
1500 PRINT "LESS CLOSING STOCK (";:LET X=SK:GOSUB 1600:PRINT ")"
1510 PRINT
1520 LET X=ABS(PL):IF PL>=0 THEN PRINT "PROFIT ";:GOSUB 1600:PRINT
1530 IF PL<0 THEN PRINT "LOSS ";:GOSUB 1600:PRINT
1540 GOSUB 1590:RETURN
1550 INPUT A$
1560 IF A$<>"Y" AND A$<>"N" THEN GOTO 1550
1570 RETURN
★ 1580 CLS:RETURN
1590 PRINT:PRINT "PRESS RETURN FOR MENU";:INPUT A$:RETURN
★ 1600 IF X<0 THEN PRINT "-";
1610 IF FF=0 AND CF=0 THEN PRINT C$;
★ 1620 LET X$=STR$(ABS(X)):LET L=LEN(X$)
1630 FOR I=6 TO 0 STEP -3
1640 LET N=L-I:IF N<=0 THEN GOTO 1680
1650 IF N>3 THEN LET N=3
★ 1660 IF I>0 THEN PRINT MID$(X$,L-(N+I-1),N);",";
★ 1670 IF I=0 THEN PRINT MID$(X$,L-(N-1),N);
1680 NEXT I
1690 IF FF=0 AND CF=1 THEN PRINT C$;
1700 RETURN
```

When you want to stop the game, type in 0 in answer to the question "How many shops . . .". It will then tell you how well you have done.

Conversions

Coffee stall program

Commodore 64: / **Vic 20:**
```
10 PRINT CHR$(147)
```

Apple:
```
10 HOME
```

Stock Market program

Commodore 64: / **Vic 20:**
```
910 PRINT CHR$(147):RETURN
```

Apple:
```
910 HOME:RETURN
```

TRS-80:
```
10 DEF FNR(X)=INT(RND(0)*X)+1
```

Spectrum*:
```
10 DEF FNR(X)=INT(RND*X)+1
250 GOSUB 340*(X=1)+370*(X=2)+400*(X=3)+430*(X=4)
730 PRINT "WHICH COMPANY":INPUT I$:LET CO=CODE(I$)-64
```

Fashion shop program

Commodore 64: / **Vic 20:**
```
1580 PRINT CHR$(147):RETURN
1625 LET L=L-1:LET X$=RIGHT$(X$,L)
```

Vic 20:
```
1600 IF POS(0)-INT(POS(0)/22)*22+LEN(STR$(X))>20
     THEN PRINT
1605 IF X<0 THEN PRINT "-";
```

Spectrum*:
```
10 DIM N$(6,10):DIM F(6,7)
190 GOSUB 210*(N=1)+1170*(N=2)+1340*(N=3)+1390*(N=4)+
    360*(N=5)
1660 IF I>0 THEN PRINT X$(L-(N+I-1) TO L-I);",";
1670 IF I=0 THEN PRINT X$(L-(N-1) TO L);
```

Apple:
```
20 LET C$="$":LET CF=0
1580 HOME:RETURN
```

TRS-80:
```
20 LET C$="$":LET CF=0
1625 LET X$=RIGHT$(X$,L-1):LET L=L-1
```

MSX:
```
1625 LET X$=RIGHT$(X$,L-1):LET L=L-1
```

*Use caps lock when you type the program in and when you run it.

Stock Market program

This program enables you to test your skills at buying and selling shares. When you run the program, you have five options shown in the chart below.

Select which option you want by pressing the letter and then RETURN or ENTER. *

P – Portfolio. Reminds you how many shares you have in each company, the price you bought them at, and the current price.

L – Prices. Gives the prices for shares in each company for this week and last week, and the change in price.

C – Cash. Shows you how much cash you have in the bank and the value of your shares.

B – Buy shares. You select a company (A-E) and type in the number of shares you want.

S – Sell shares. You select a company (A-E) and type in the number you wish to sell.

You can do as much trading as you want during each week. When you have finished trading, press E and RETURN or ENTER to end the week.

★
```
10 DEF FNR(X)=INT(RND(1)*X)+1
20 GOSUB 920:GOSUB 810
30 PRINT:PRINT "P/C/B/S/L/E/Q":INPUT A$
40 IF A$="L" THEN GOSUB 810
50 IF A$="P" THEN GOSUB 860
60 IF A$="C" THEN GOSUB 770
70 IF A$="B" THEN GOSUB 640
80 IF A$="S" THEN GOSUB 690
90 IF A$="E" THEN GOSUB 120
100 IF A$<>"Q" THEN GOTO 30
110 STOP
120 GOSUB 910:PRINT "END OF WEEK ";W;" NEWS":PRINT
130 LET W=W+1:IF W=53 THEN LET W=1
140 LET RF=0:IF FNR(10)>7 THEN GOSUB 320
150 IF FNR(10)>9 THEN LET IT=SGN(8.1-IR)
160 IF IR<5 OR IR>11 THEN LET IR=IR+SGN(8-IR)
170 LET C=C+INT((C*IR/100)/52):LET HF=0
180 FOR I=1 TO 5:LET L(I)=P(I):NEXT I
190 IF TF=2 THEN GOSUB 500:LET HF=1
200 IF TF=1 THEN GOSUB 460
210 FOR I=1 TO NC:IF W=D(I) THEN GOSUB 470:LET HF=1
220 IF W=D(I)+1 THEN GOSUB 530:LET HF=1
230 NEXT I
240 LET I=FNR(NC):LET X=FNR(15):IF X>4 OR HF=1 THEN
    GOTO 260
```
★
```
250 ON X GOSUB 340,370,400,430
260 LET TS=0:FOR I=1 TO NC
270 LET P(I)=INT(P(I)+T(I)+FNR(I*2)-1)
280 LET C(I)=P(I)-L(I):LET TS=TS+S(I)*P(I)
290 LET X(I)=X(I)+1:IF X(I)=W(I) THEN GOSUB 590
300 NEXT I
310 PRINT:PRINT "PRESS RETURN FOR NEXT WEEK":INPUT A$:GOSUB 810:RETURN
320 PRINT "* INTEREST RATE CHANGES BY ";IT;"%"
330 PRINT:LET IR=IR+IT:LET RF=1:RETURN
340 PRINT "* COMPANY ";C$(I);" GETS NEW CONTRACT":PRINT
350 LET X=10+FNR(10):LET Y=FNR(3)+3
360 LET X(I)=0:GOSUB 620:RETURN
370 PRINT "* COMPANY ";C$(I);" LOSES BIG CONTRACT":PRINT
380 LET X=-30-FNR(20):LET Y=-FNR(3)-3
390 LET X(I)=0:GOSUB 620:RETURN
400 PRINT "* COMPANY ";C$(I);" DIRECTOR RESIGNS":PRINT
410 LET X=-10-FNR(10):LET Y=-FNR(3)-3
420 LET X(I)=0:GOSUB 620:RETURN
```

What can affect the price of shares?

★ The banks' interest rate may change. If it falls, the share price may go up. If it rises, the price may go down.

★ A company may win a contract, making its shares go up.

★ A company may lose a large contract, and its share price will fall.

★ If the director of company resigns, this will have a bad effect on its shares.

★ Rumours of a take-over bid will cause shares of the target company to rise in price. If the take-over does not after all occur, then the price will go down.

★ If a company is about to announce its profits and share out its dividends, prices will go up. When the profits are announced, they will be described as good, average or bad. Your dividend and the price change will depend on the result, although the general trend will be a price drop once the dividends have been distributed.

See page 43 for conversions.

```
430 IF TF>0 THEN RETURN
440 PRINT "* TAKE-OVER RUMOUR AT COMPANY ";C$(I):PRINT:LET TF=1:LET X=10
450 LET Y=FNR(3):GOSUB 620:LET TC=I:RETURN
460 LET TF=2:LET X=5:LET Y=FNR(3):LET I=TC:GOSUB 620:RETURN
470 PRINT "* COMPANY ";C$(I);" ABOUT TO ANNOUNCE":PRINT "PROFITS AND SHARE"
480 PRINT "OUT DIVIDENDS":PRINT
490 LET X=10:LET Y=0:GOSUB 620:RETURN
500 LET X=FNR(2):IF X=1 THEN PRINT "* TAKE-OVER AT COMPANY ";C$(TC):PRINT
510 IF X=2 THEN LET I=TC:LET X=-15:LET Y=-FNR(2):GOSUB 620
520 LET TF=0:RETURN
530 LET X=FNR(10):PRINT "* COMPANY ";C$(I);" PROFITS ARE ";
540 IF X<4 THEN PRINT "GOOD":LET D=20
550 IF X>7 THEN PRINT "BAD":LET D=0
560 IF X<8 AND X>3 THEN PRINT "AVERAGE":LET D=10
570 LET X=-X:LET Y=-FNR(3):GOSUB 620:LET D=INT((D/100)*S(I)*P(I))
580 PRINT "YOU GET DIVIDEND OF ";D:LET C=C+D:RETURN
590 LET X(I)=0
600 IF T(I)=0 THEN LET Y=FNR(10)-5:LET W(I)=FNR(3)+1:GOSUB 630:RETURN
610 LET T(I)=0:LET W(I)=FNR(3)+3:RETURN
620 LET P(I)=INT(P(I)+(X/100)*P(I))
630 LET T(I)=P(I)*(Y/100):RETURN
640 GOSUB 730:GOSUB 760:IF (P(CO)*NS)>C THEN PRINT "CASH?":GOTO 640
650 IF NS>0 THEN LET B(CO)=INT((B(CO)*S(CO)+P(CO)*NS)/(S(CO)+NS))
660 LET S(CO)=S(CO)+NS
670 LET TS=TS+P(CO)*NS:LET C=C-P(CO)*NS-INT(0.03*P(CO)*NS)
680 GOSUB 860:RETURN
690 GOSUB 730:GOSUB 760:IF NS>S(CO) THEN PRINT "WHAT?":GOTO 690
700 LET C=C+P(CO)*NS-INT(0.03*P(CO)*NS):LET S(CO)=S(CO)-NS
710 IF S(CO)=0 THEN LET B(CO)=0
720 LET TS=TS-P(CO)*NS:GOSUB 860:RETURN
★ 730 PRINT "WHICH COMPANY":INPUT I$:LET CO=ASC(I$)-64
740 IF CO<1 OR CO>NC THEN GOTO 730
750 RETURN
760 PRINT "HOW MANY SHARES":INPUT NS:RETURN
770 GOSUB 910:PRINT:PRINT "FINANCE:":PRINT
780 PRINT "CASH : ";C:PRINT "(INCLUDES INTEREST"
790 PRINT "AT ";INT(IR);"%":PRINT "SHARES WORTH : ";TS
800 PRINT "TOTAL : ";TS+C:RETURN
810 GOSUB 910:PRINT:PRINT "PRICES: WEEK ";W:PRINT
820 PRINT " CO. LW. TW. CH.":PRINT " --- --- --- ---"
830 PRINT:FOR I=1 TO NC
840 PRINT TAB(1);C$(I);TAB(6);L(I);TAB(11);P(I);TAB(16);C(I)
850 NEXT I:RETURN
860 GOSUB 910:PRINT:PRINT "PORTFOLIO":PRINT
870 PRINT " CO. NO. BP. TP.":PRINT " --- --- --- ---"
880 PRINT:FOR I=1 TO NC
890 PRINT TAB(1);C$(I);TAB(6);S(I);TAB(11);B(I);TAB(16);P(I)
900 NEXT I:RETURN
★ 910 CLS:RETURN
920 LET NC=5
930 DIM C$(5):DIM P(NC):DIM L(NC):DIM T(NC)
940 DIM C(NC):DIM S(NC):DIM B(NC):DIM W(NC):DIM X(NC):DIM D(NC)
950 LET C=FNR(NC):FOR I=1 TO NC:LET C$(I)=CHR$(64+I)
960 LET P(I)=100*I-50+FNR(5):LET T(I)=0
970 LET L(I)=P(I)-FNR(3)+2:LET C(I)=P(I)-L(I)
980 LET W(I)=FNR(3)+2:LET X(I)=FNR(2)
990 LET C=C+1:IF C>NC THEN LET C=1
1000 LET D(C)=I*5:NEXT I
1010 LET IR=10:LET IT=-1:LET C=2500
1020 LET TS=0:LET W=1:LET TF=0:LET TC=0:RETURN
```

Each week's news will be shown on the screen.

Glossary

Accountant. A qualified person who specializes in bookkeeping, auditing annual accounts and financial advice.

Asset. Anything of value owned by a company or individual e.g. equipment or stock. Also intangible things such as patents.

Balance sheet. A statement of the assets and liabilities of a company at a particular time.

Bankrupt. The state of a person who has more debts than he can pay and therefore is judged by a court to be insolvent.

Bartering. Doing business by exchanging.

Brokers. Agents through whom people buy and sell shares.

Budget. A financial plan.

Cash flow. The flow of money into and out of a business.

Closing stock. The amount of unsold goods you have at the end of an accounting period.

Company. An organization created for a specific purpose, which has a separate legal identity from the people who combine to form it.

Credit. An allowance of time to repay a debt.

Creditor. A person or company to whom money is owed.

Current assets. Cash and other assets such as stock which are sold in the normal course of trading.

Current liabilities. Debts which fall due in a relatively short period.

Debt. An amount owed.

Debtor. A person or company that owes money.

Delivery note. A note attached to goods when they are delivered specifying what they are.

Depreciation. The decrease in value of equipment due to use or lapse of time.

Direct mail. A method of selling goods or services direct from supplier to customer by sending sales literature through the post.

Direct selling. Selling direct to the public.

Director. A member of a board of directors who make the policy decisions for a company.

Discount. A deduction from the normal selling price, usually worked out as a percentage of the normal price.

Dividend. A proportion of a company's profits which is paid to the shareholders.

Exporting. Selling goods abroad.

Grant. A gift of money given for a specific purpose.

Guarantor. Someone who guarantees to pay a person's debts if that person cannot.

Interest. The money paid by a borrower for the use of the lender's money.

International company. A company which operates mainly from one country but exports elsewhere.

Invoice. A bill.

Jobbers. Dealers in shares on the London Stock Market.

Liabilities. Money a business owes, both externally (e.g. creditors, overdraft) and internally (e.g. shareholders' capital).

Limited company. A company where the shareholders' liability is limited to the amount they have paid for the shares.

Liquidation. A legal process whereby the life of a company is brought to an end.

Mail order. Advertising goods and selling them by post. (See also Direct mail.)

Manufacturing. The process of making goods.

Marketing. Activities concerned with finding and maintaining markets for a firm's goods or services.

Merger. The joining of two or more companies to form a new company. (See also Take-over).

Monopoly. The only company dealing in certain goods or services.

Multinational company. A company with factories and offices in many different countries.

Official receiver. An official appointed by a court to look after the affairs of a bankrupt person or to supervise the compulsory winding up of a company.

Opening stock. The amount of unsold stock at the beginning of a financial period.

Overdraft. A bank loan in which the customer's current account is allowed to go into debt to an agreed limit. Interest is calculated on a daily basis.

Overhead. A cost incurred in the normal running of a business which is not directly concerned with the product or service.

Partnership. A group of people trading as one company.

Predator. A company about to take over another.

Profit. The difference between the cost of providing goods or services, and a higher price at which you sell them.

Profit and loss account. A financial statement showing a business' profit or loss over a given period.

Public company. A company whose shares can be offered to the general public and traded on a Stock Exchange.

Purchase order. A form used for ordering goods.

Rates. An annual tax on the value of a property.

Retailer. Shopkeeper.

Retained profit. Profit which is kept in a business.

Sales tax. A tax charged in some countries on the shop price of certain goods.

Security. A valuable possession which you promise to sell in order to pay debts which you would otherwise be unable to pay.

Share capital. The amount of money invested in a company by its shareholders.

Shareholder. The owner of a share or shares in a company, entitling the shareholder to vote at company meetings and to a share in the profits.

Sole trader. A person with sole responsibility for a company's affairs.

Stock. The quantity of materials and finished goods held by a business.

Stock control. Procedures for trying to maintain optimum levels of stock.

Stock Exchange. Also called Stock Market. Place where shares can be bought and sold.

Take-over. Gaining control of a company by buying a majority of its shares.

Target. A company about to be taken over.

Target mailing. Selling by direct mail by sending sales literature to a specific group of people.

Tax. A sum of money collected by governments from businesses and private individuals to pay for public services.

Trading. Buying and selling goods and services for a profit.

Turnover. The total sales income of a business in a given period.

Value Added Tax (VAT). A tax charged in certain countries (including the UK) on the purchase price of goods and services.

Answers

Page 4
A retailer buys goods (e.g. meat, cheese, cereal) in large quantities, cuts them up and sells them in smaller quantities.

Page 9
Sasha's dressmaking
The labour costs, own wages and overheads total 1,900 tokens, i.e. almost 12.7 tokens per dress. Material costs for each dress come to 11 tokens. So the total cost of each dress is 23.7 tokens. Sasha would therefore make a profit of 1.3 tokens.

Page 11
The large amount of money going out in the first month is the sum spent on equipment and so on.

Page 17
Profit and loss chart for Monsieur Dupont
IN
Sales 1,500
OUT
Expenditure 800
Depreciation 20
Opening stock 80
Less closing stock ....(100)
Profit 700

Page 18
The retained profit would be 2,500.

Page 23
Judge for yourself
1. No; Alan has not yet left the shop.
2. Because Martin has worn them, the shoes cannot be sold to anyone else. Since the complaint is not to do with the quality of the goods, he cannot demand a refund.
3. The shopkeeper is wrong. He should exchange the goods or refund the money, and then take up the matter with the manufacturer himself.

Page 24
Value Added Tax
1. Sue pays the government £2.25 minus the £1.50 she paid to her suppliers = 75p.
2. Harry adds £9 to his bill of £60 for actually painting the room, plus £4.50 for VAT on the paint. So the total VAT added to the bill is £13.50.

Index